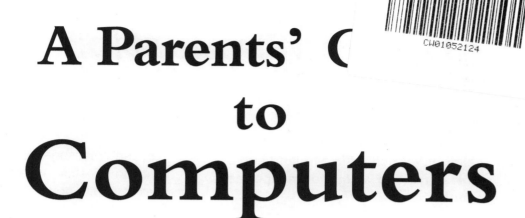

A Parents' Guide to Computers

Key Stages 1 and 2

Sharon Harrison

Illustrated by Sascha Lipscomb

Contents

Hodder Children's Books

The only home learning programme supported by the NCPTA

Introduction

This book is for those who:

- ✧ **Have a child aged between 5 and 11 years old at school in England and Wales, in either a state or independent school.**
- ✧ **Want to know how the new ICT curriculum will affect how their child is taught at school.**
- ✧ **Use a computer at work or at home (or intend to buy one) and want to help their child learn computer skills.**

WHY IS IT IMPORTANT FOR PRIMARY-AGED CHILDREN TO LEARN COMPUTER SKILLS?

Computers are now an indispensable part of our everyday lives and, as the millennium bug panic showed us, many important services are dependent on them. By the time today's primary-school children are adults, using a computer confidently will be an essential life-skill – as important as reading, writing and maths.

Opening up the world

As well as ensuring that children are properly prepared for adult life, computer skills also offer children exciting new ways of learning. Access to the Internet has opened up the world – children can send messages around the globe, use email to question experts and scientists, track their favourite pop personalities, or go on a 'virtual tour' of a museum or gallery. The opportunities are boundless.

THE NATIONAL GRID FOR LEARNING

In the late 1990s, the government launched the National Grid for Learning programme. This aims to ensure that: 'high-quality educational material will be available on the Internet and that children and teachers are confident users of computers to make use of the grid content.' To become confident users, all children must be taught to understand computers, to use different computer programs, and to apply computer technology to all school subjects.

Before children can use computers properly, they need to learn the basic skills, step-by-step. Teaching the key computer skills at primary school will give children the opportunity to learn more widely as well as equip them to use computers independently at secondary school and beyond.

USING THIS BOOK

This book is designed to be dipped into – you can find the sections you want from the contents list. Words in the text printed in **bold type** are explained in the glossary on page 31. Most activities in the book are based on Microsoft programs and other commonly used software, but all can be adapted. 'He' and 'she' are used alternately throughout this book but all references apply to either sex. For further contacts and information sources, look in the Useful resources section on pages 29-30.

The computer curriculum

Computer education in schools is called **Information and Communications Technology (ICT). It requires that children are taught how to use computers and the Internet and also other equipment, such as printers, scanners, digital cameras and simple robots.**

The revised National Curriculum for ICT was introduced in 2000. What has to be taught is organised under the following headings:

1. Finding things out.
2. Developing ideas and making things happen.
3. Exchanging and sharing information.
4. Reviewing, modifying and evaluating work as it progresses.

Schools can follow detailed lesson plans published by the Qualifications and Curriculum Agency (see page 30 for the website address).

WHAT CAN YOU EXPECT YOUR CHILD TO LEARN IN KEY STAGE 1?

Children aged 5-7 will be given the chance to use a range of different **software** such as **word processors**, **art programs**, interactive or **adventure programs**, encyclopaedia and dictionary **CD-ROMs**, **graph and chart programs**, and **floor robots**. They should discuss how computers are used in everyday life and begin to understand some of the things that computers can and cannot do.

1. Examples of finding things out

Your child will learn to:

- ❑ Use a CD-ROM game or 'talking book', where he must click on different pictures, words or buttons to move through and explore the program.
- ❑ Use a CD-ROM encyclopaedia, working his way through the **menus** to find information about animals, for example.

- ❑ Collect information on a topic such as his favourite foods, and enter the information on to a simple computer chart.

2. Examples of developing ideas and making things happen

Your child will learn to:

- ❑ Use a computer mouse confidently to click on buttons and move objects on a computer screen. For example, he might dress a teddy by choosing clothes in the right order, or match and place word labels to parts of the body.
- ❑ Use a word processor to write his name, then simple sentences. He will also learn to **save** and print out his work.
- ❑ Use a drawing and painting program to create a picture in a style that makes good use of the program's basic features, e.g. by drawing thick lines and filling in the spaces with bold colours.

- ❑ Key in the correct instructions to move a toy robot around the floor, or a computer 'creature' around the screen.
- ❑ Play an adventure game that involves solving maths puzzles.

3. Examples of exchanging and sharing information

❑ Think about how to display his computer work, e.g. deciding to use large, easy-read print for a story written for a little brother or sister.

❑ Understand the different ways he can present work on the computer, e.g. text only, or pictures and computer sound.

4. Examples of reviewing, modifying and evaluating work

❑ Reading what he has typed, making changes and correcting mistakes such as missing full stops.

❑ Drawing a picture in a graphics program and changing the colours to see if it looks better.

WHAT CAN YOU EXPECT YOUR CHILD TO LEARN IN KEY STAGE 2?

In the years from 7-11 you should expect your child to progress from KS1, developing more skills in using word processors, **databases** and art and music programs. Children will also move on to using **spreadsheets**, **multimedia programs**, **email** and the **Internet**, and learn a simple type of **programming**. Here are examples of the key things your child should be taught:

1. Finding things out
How to

❑ Use a computer to search for information on a subject, e.g. on the Internet, or a CD-ROM.

❑ Collect and organise information sensibly and put it into a database.

❑ Search a database logically and check that the results are realistic.

2. Developing ideas and making things happen
How to

❑ Combine writing, graphs and pictures (e.g. in posters and newspaper pages) and improve as necessary.

❑ Create a multimedia presentation using text, pictures and sound.

❑ Create, test and improve simple programs for, e.g. drawing geometric shapes on the screen.

❑ Use a spreadsheet for tasks such as budgeting for an end-of-term party.

> At KS2 children should get the chance to use a wider variety of computer equipment as well as software. They should also be finding out more about, and comparing the uses of, ICT inside and outside school.

3. Exchanging and sharing information
How to

❑ Choose the best way to communicate information, e.g. by displaying printed work, recording words or music, or by sending emails.

❑ Adapt how the work is presented depending on the audience, e.g. parents, friends, or younger children.

4. Reviewing, modifying and evaluating work in progress
How to

❑ Evaluate and develop work in progress and understand that a computer lets you redraft and improve work more easily.

❑ Discuss the differences between using a computer and other ways of doing a particular task.

The computer graph is neater but the whole class can see the big wall graph!

USING COMPUTERS TO TEACH LITERACY

Schools now teach English during the daily Literacy Hour and many will be using computers to help and extend their teaching. The literacy curriculum suggests that children should use ICT to:

 ✧ Draft and improve writing.

 ✧ Present work more effectively.

 ✧ Develop reading and research skills and improve spelling.

Here are some typical uses of ICT in literacy activities that are used through the primary years:

❑ Book making and learning to draft and improve writing

When a child writes a story on the word processor, he can:

 ❑ Break it up into manageable stages, concentrating first on his ideas and not on spelling and punctuation.
 ❑ Save and print the first draft, read it through and check for mistakes.
 ❑ Talk about the vocabulary he has used and think of more descriptive words.
 ❑ Produce the final version and add a picture he has drawn or selected from a **clip-art** file on the computer.

❑ Writing newspaper reports

In a sequence of lessons, children will:

 ❑ Look at real newspaper articles and headlines.
 ❑ Talk about the journalistic style of writing and plan the layout and design of their article on paper.
 ❑ Set up the layout on a word processor or desktop publishing program, e.g. three text columns, a picture box and headline banner.
 ❑ Draft the story, adjusting the length to fit and think about how to convey the information to the reader using bullet points, boxes and tables as well as altering the style, size and colour of headlines and titles.

❑ Learning research skills using CD-ROM encyclopaedias, databases and the Internet

Learning to find their way through non-fiction and reference materials is an important literacy skill. Children must:

 ❑ Learn to scan the menus and indexes to search through a CD-ROM and (at KS2) Internet **websites**.
 ❑ Practice making notes about the information they find.
 ❑ Learn to **save** documents into **folders** on the computer.

Can you think of a better word than 'nice' to describe the dog?

❏ Developing reading and spelling skills, and understanding sentence structure

Some schools use software to develop reading skills. A good example is *Sherlock* (from Topologika) in which children work together on a piece of writing with many hidden letters and words. They work out the missing words from a range of reading clues such as the length of the word, its position in the sentence, and the context of the rest of the passage, e.g:

> **Rosie peered th_ _ _ _ _ the letter- _ _ _ in the huge green _ _ _ _**

❏ Using a computer spell-checker

Your child will need to learn how to use a spell-checker carefully and to understand that the computer will not know *all* the words (e.g. names) or be able to correct mistakes such as using 'there' instead of 'their'.

Parents may worry that a spell-checker will make their children lazy spellers. In fact, the opposite seems to be true. Most spell-checkers highlight the suspect word in colour, alerting a child each time he mis-spells a word. He then needs to stop and choose the correct spelling from the computer's list of suggestions.

❏ Multimedia presentation and web authoring

Older children might make a multimedia presentation on a school trip. This involves creating inter-linked screen pages containing text, pictures, sounds, photos and even short pieces of video footage. Clicking the mouse on different parts of the screen starts an animation or sound sequence, opens a picture or text window, or moves to a new page.

USING COMPUTERS TO TEACH NUMERACY

From 1999, a new National Numeracy Strategy proposed changes in the ways in which maths is taught in primary schools. Part of the Strategy encourages the use of ICT to support children's learning, in particular using data handling and problem-solving software. Here are some examples of typical computer activities:

❏ Understanding measurement and angles, and learning to put instructions in a logical order

Your child will probably use a version of a programming language called LOGO, which is used in many university departments. This simplified version helps children to solve maths problems using a step-by-step mathematical approach.

Key Stage 1 activities:

- ❏ Program a floor robot to move forward, backward, right and left.
- ❏ Practise adding and subtracting by following a list of instructions, e.g. understanding that '*forward 4, forward 3*' will move the robot the same distance as '*forward 7*'.

Key Stage 2 activities:

❑ Learn about shapes and angles

Use what you know about the sides and angles of a square to make an on-screen robot (or 'turtle'). Draw a square. Use the right programming instructions, as follows:

forward 10 (steps)*, right 90* (degrees)

forward 10 (steps)*, right 90* (degrees)

forward 10 (steps)*, right 90* (degrees)

forward 10 (steps)*, right 90* (degrees)

❑ Thinking ahead and planning

Draw a pattern in LOGO by rotating a square. Break down the task into simple stages.

Handling data

Key Stage 1 activities

❑ Learn to display information with a simple graphing program.

❑ Discuss how quickly the computer can do a task and think about the best choice of chart or graph for their data.

Key Stage 2 activities

❑ Develop skills in displaying information in a more sophisticated graph or chart, e.g. as a bar chart, pie chart, or line graph.

Number of skips we could do without stopping

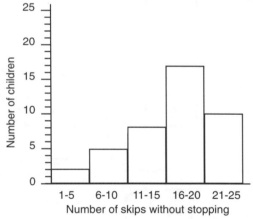

Question: How many children scored more than 15 skips?

❑ Learn how data is organised using a simple database.

A class may make a database with a record for each child containing information such as age, height, weight, foot size, and so on. They would then search the database to find out the average height of the class, or whether taller children have larger feet.

The computer curriculum

Later on, when children understand how a simple database works, they can compare large sets of data in an established database. They might search a database on road safety to find answers to questions such as: 'Do more accidents happen in the winter months?'.

Problem solving and patterns with numbers

Teachers find that computer spreadsheet programs can help children to understand basic ideas in algebra, as well as using 'the four rules' (+ − x ÷) to solve problems.

Key Stage 2 activities:

❑ Put a number in a spreadsheet formula, work out the answer in your head, then check it against the spreadsheet calculation.

❑ Put a sequence of numbers into the formula, e.g. 1, 2, 3, . . . and look for a pattern in the sequence of numbers that 'come out'.

❑ Use a spreadsheet to plan the end-of-term party. List the food and drink for the party, enter the cost of each item and make the spreadsheet calculate the total.

Understanding numbers and practising calculations

Teachers may use specially designed numeracy programs for teaching particular mathematical ideas, place value in hundreds, tens and units. Arithmetic practice programs give children the opportunity to increase their calculation skills.

1000	2000	3000	4000	5000	6000	7000	8000	9000
100	200	300	400	500	600	700	800	900
10	20	30	40	50	60	70	80	90
1	2	3	4	5	6	7	8	9
0.1	0.2	0.3	0.4	0.5	0.6	0.7	0.8	0.9

2 6 3 1 . 7

two thousand six hundred and thirty one point seven
(from *Developing Numbers* by ATM)

USING COMPUTERS IN OTHER SUBJECTS

Science

✧ A wealth of CD-ROMs is available to support the science curriculum at KS1 and 2 in schools. Children can research topics such as the human body, animal habitats, the weather or magnetism.

✧ At KS2, children connect sensors to a computer to record changes in light and temperature. Datalogging software takes automatic readings at regular intervals and builds up a graph of the changes.

✧ Children at KS2 may use databases and spreadsheet programs to record the results of experiments, such as how changing the angle of a slope affects the time it takes for a toy car to roll down it.

✧ The computer will calculate averages and display results in a graph.

History and geography

❑ Some schools have transferred information on the 1890s census for their local area into a computer database. Children learning about the Victorians are able to call up original records and search for the people who lived in a particular road, or had the same surname as themselves.

❑ United Nations' world statistics are available on a database. Children can investigate topics such as lifestyles in different countries, finding out how many doctors, teachers or cars each country has per 1000 people.

❑ Many excellent, interactive CD-ROMs can add an extra dimension to history or geography. For example, children can use a simulation program about a rainforest to learn what happens if they change the balance of nature by cutting down part of it. Children can also explore life in another age using a CD-ROM that presents information through video clips, sound tracks, photographs and text, and encourages interaction by answering questions that are typed in.

Come and find out what we do at School.

Design and technology

At KS2 your child might use a computer to animate a model she has built from a construction kit or from wood and card. For example, she might build a model lighthouse and connect it to a control box linked to the computer. She would then write a simple computer program to make the bulb flash and even to send Morse code light signals.

Control Box

Art

Many schools use graphics packages to give children the chance to experiment with line and colour. Children can try out different colour combinations easily as well as being able to change what they don't like.

Your child might:

- ◇ Look at paintings which have simple shapes and solid colours (e.g. by Picasso or Matisse) and create a computer picture in a similar style.
- ◇ Design a wallpaper motif and repeat it to create a pattern.
- ◇ Produce a 'still life', using the reflection facility in a painting program to draw a symmetrical bowl.

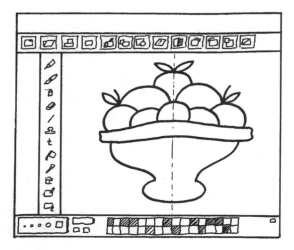

- ◇ Search a CD-ROM of National Gallery paintings to find examples of pictures by a particular artist.

Music

Children might use a computer program to compose short pieces of electronic music which can then be combined with traditional instruments.

USING THE INTERNET IN SCHOOL

The Internet is an outstanding resource for schools. Generally, children begin to use it in KS2. They may start learning about the system by sending emails to each other within the school's own network.

Net or email pals

Your child's school may link with another school in the UK, or in a different country, and pair up children as email pals. This is an exciting way to develop language and writing skills and to learn geography as well as to develop ICT skills.

Remind your child:

When you email a net-pal:
- ◇ Never give your address or telephone number.
- ◇ Never arrange to meet anyone in person.

Children will also learn to access the Internet and search for information with a **web browser**. As surfing the net can eat up curriculum time, teachers often earmark suitable websites, saving the addresses in the web browser '**bookmarks**' or '**favourites**' facility for children to access directly.

A word of warning

Information posted on the Internet is not regulated and it is possible to find material which is both offensive and illegal. As a safeguard, each school should have a screened Internet service to prevent children from getting through to such sites. In addition, many will operate an Internet Policy where children only ever use the Internet with adult supervision. A written home-school agreement, in which the child agrees not to misuse the facility, is another way of ensuring that everyone realises the importance of using the Internet responsibly.

Computers in schools

When computers were first introduced into primary schools in the 1980s they were expensive items. The (usually) one computer was timetabled to be shared between all the classrooms. As costs came down, schools were able to buy more computers, and today nearly all schools have the equivalent of one computer per classroom, while more and more are setting up dedicated ICT rooms.

⬦ **One or more computers per classroom**
A teacher may introduce an activity to the whole class, and then organise a rota over a period of days or weeks so that each child will have a turn using the computer.

⬦ **Computer rooms**
Many primary schools are setting up rooms equipped with about 15 computers. Schools are also investing in computer-video projectors. These enable teachers to show how programs work by projecting an image of the computer screen on to a large wall screen or an 'interactive' whiteboard. The teacher can control the program with a pointer and can also write on this type of board.

⬦ **Learning**
Classes will have at least one ICT lesson a week. Where children are learning specific computer skills, there may be one child per computer. For discussion and problem-solving, two children might work together.

⬦ **Laptop computers**
In primary schools with no space for a computer room, one option is to build up a set of portable or laptop computers that can be used on tables in the classrooms. National research projects carried out in the 1990s showed that this system was very effective in raising standards in ICT, particularly where schools used the portable computers for homework. However, security and maintenance standards have to be high.

⬦ **Future changes**
As the cost of computers falls, many schools may aim to have a central computer room, a few computers in each classroom and a set of laptop computers. In the race to keep up with technology, schools will have to replace their computers every five years.

Helping at school

You may already be helping to buy computer equipment by collecting supermarket or newspaper vouchers. Schools depend on parents to organise fundraising events or to find sponsorship to build up their computer facilities. Most primary schools also welcome parental help in the classroom. Get in touch with the school's ICT coordinator via your child's teacher if you would like to help with computer work.

If you are computer-confident you might be asked to:

- ✧ Help one or more children use the mouse and with a word processor keyboard.
- ✧ Supervise a group accessing the **Internet**. The teacher will explain what she wants you to do but do ask if you are unsure about anything.

When you help in the classroom remember to:

- ✧ Find out exactly what the teacher wants the children to learn.
- ✧ Be patient and explain rather than show how to do a task.
- ✧ Encourage children to think and work things out for themselves.
- ✧ Make sure you know and keep to the school policy on using the Internet.

- ✧ Monitor carefully what appears on the screen.
- ✧ Report any unsuitable **websites** to the teacher or ICT coordinator.

If you are less confident with your computer skills you can still help by:

- ✧ Freeing the teacher to work with the group on the computers by giving help elsewhere in the class. You can also give learning support in reading on-screen information and finding the correct keys.

SCHOOL COMPUTER CLUBS

If the school has no computer club and you are a confident computer-user, then you could offer to help set one up.

Here are some examples of computer-club activities:

- ✧ Helping with homework, using the Internet and **CD-ROMs**.
- ✧ Creating and maintaining a school website.
- ✧ Producing a multimedia presentation for parents' evening.

Choosing a home computer

If you are planning to buy a computer for your child, it is worth spending time investigating the most suitable package for your family needs. Here are some issues to consider:

PC OR MAC?

Similar software is available for both IBM compatible **PCs** and **Apple Macintosh** computers. If the computer is mainly for your child's use, you will probably want to choose whichever type she uses at school.

> You can walk into a 'computer superstore' and buy a computer off the shelf, or you can order one by phone from one of the many companies who sell directly by mail order. But remember that these companies only sell their own or a limited range of products and will not give you independent advice. So, before buying, look through the computer magazines where you will see a full range of products and suppliers, read the reviews and compare costs. Also talk to friends who have recently taken the plunge.

MULTIMEDIA

Make sure you choose a multimedia computer, i.e. with sound and graphic facilities, and one with the fastest **processor speed** and largest **memory** you can sensibly afford. To always run the latest **software**, you will need to replace your computer every five years or so, just as schools will. Upgrading a computer to have a bigger memory can be a cheap alternative to replacement, but requires expert advice.

Invest in:

❏ A large monitor, at least 17". This makes a world of difference when you and your child are working together at the computer. Text and graphics are bigger, more impressive and easier to read.

❏ A microphone to record sounds, voices and music.

❏ A colour printer for art and design work (but do check the cost of the replacement inks).

Think about buying:

❏ Headphones, so that computer sound will not disturb other family members while your child listens to a talking story or plays a noisy computer game.

❏ A small mouse which is easier for an infant-aged child to control. They do not cost much and are sold by many computer companies – see page 29 for list.

❏ For art programs, a graphics tablet with an electronic pen. This is easier to draw with than a mouse or tracker ball.

❏ An inexpensive scanner, for scanning photos and pictures to use in art and design work.

SPECIAL NEEDS

A range of specialist **hardware** and software is available for children with special educational needs or disabilities, e.g. switches, alternative keyboards and voice-recognition software. Several companies supply this type of specialist equipment and software to schools (see page 29 for suppliers).

Activities at home: the basics

To help your child at home you need not be an expert, but basic computer know-how is useful along with some understanding of the programs you are using. If you are a beginner, remember that you and your child can enjoy learning together.

LEARNING TOGETHER

It is very important to talk with your child about what you are doing together on the computer and what you are both trying to learn. Your support is as important as the **software** you use or the task you choose.

- ✧ Be patient. Show your child what to do without doing it for her.

- ✧ Be positive. Give lots of praise and expect mistakes.

- ✧ Relax – it is really quite hard to do permanent damage to the computer or software.

SOFTWARE

Most home computers come with a standard package of software. For a typical IBM compatible **PC** you are likely to get a **software bundle**, such as Microsoft *Works/Office* or Lotus *SmartSuite*. These contain a range of key programs: a **word processor** (e.g. Microsoft *Word*), a **spreadsheet** (e.g. Microsoft *Excel*), and possibly a **database** (e.g. Microsoft *Access*), and a multimedia presentation (e.g. Microsoft *PowerPoint*). An **Apple Mac** computer comes with a similar range of programs.

> In this and the following sections, most examples are based on widely used Microsoft programs. Schools often have child-friendly versions of these programs.

GENERAL COMPUTER SKILLS

Most computers come with the basic programs already installed. You should keep the program disks and CDs safe as a back-up. After following the instructions to set up your computer, you should find the icons for these programs on the desktop screen. To start or load a program, just double-click on its name or icon.

Do use the 'on-line' help facility in the programs – you will usually find the help menu on the top menu bar.

Click and double click

The first skill your child needs to practice is clicking and double-clicking the mouse button. Show her how to grasp the mouse firmly and move it slowly. Remember that you can adjust the mouse sensitivity and slow down the speed that the pointer moves across the screen.

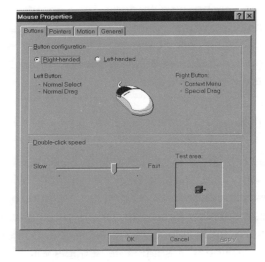

If your child is left-handed, make sure the mouse is on the left side of the computer. Many left-handers are quite happy to use the mouse as it is, but you can **configure** the buttons (see the **menu**) so that she can click the button nearest her forefinger.

If she has difficulty with double clicking, try a single click followed by tapping the enter key. You can also think about investing in a 'mini mouse' for little hands (see page 29).

Starting up and shutting down

As she gains confidence, show her how to start up the computer and find and load the program she wants to use. Show her the steps for shutting down the computer.

Windows and scrolling

Show your child how to scroll up and down a page by clicking and dragging the scroll bars. Then show her how to make windows larger or smaller, using the top right-hand buttons.

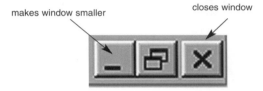

makes window smaller

closes window

GOLDEN RULES

Saving

Explain that the computer will 'forget' a new piece of work if you shut down without saving it on to the **hard disk** first. Emphasise the importance of saving work often and help your

child choose informative names for her own **files**, e.g. 'letter to Auntie Ann'.

Filing

Show your child how to keep her individual files in named **folders** so that they are easy to find next time.

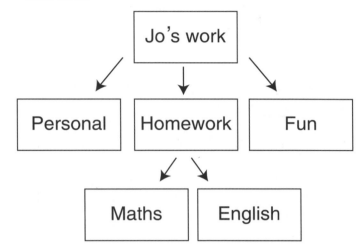

Backing up

Teach her how to back up work on a **floppy disk** regularly so that it is not lost if the computer breaks down.

Activities at home: English

The following activities are fun to do with your child, and will develop skills in English. You can pitch them at your child's level and encourage him to express his ideas in speech and writing.

SHARING CD-ROM 'TALKING BOOKS' FOR AGES 4–7

Interactive or 'talking' books can help your child learn to read. He will enjoy them because not only can he both read and listen to a story, but he can also click on the pictures and start an animation or hear a sound. To get the best from an interactive book, try this:

- ❑ Listen to the text being read by the computer and then read it through together.
- ❑ Play 'say and click': you point to a word on the screen and your child tries to read it. He then clicks on the word to check if he's right.
- ❑ Talk about what might come next in the story (or what happens next if you've already read it once).
- ❑ Talk about the pictures on the screen and what might happen if he clicks on different parts of the picture. (You will find that different characters or objects in the picture will become animated, some will talk or sing.)

MAKING BOOKS FOR AGES 5–6

Use a **word processor** to make simple books together and develop your child's writing skills. Think up a story together and help your child to type in one sentence on a page. Check and correct the spelling together and print it out. Your child can then draw a picture on each page.

Remember to show him how to use the **menu** buttons or 'icons' to **save** the story on to the **hard disk** and how to print it out.

Writing in different languages

Many people speak more than one language at home. If your child can speak and read a language other than English, look for software that gives you the font for your language(s) (e.g. *Global Writer*, available from Lingua).

MAKING BOOKS FOR AGES 7-8

- ❑ Work on longer books with a few sentences per page.
- ❑ Save and print out the first draft and get your child to read through and correct the errors on paper.
- ❑ Load up the **file**, make changes and print out the second version.
- ❑ Encourage your child to think of alternatives to over-used adjectives such as nice, good, lovely, bad, etc.
- ❑ Teach him to use the spell-checker carefully and to realise that it will not pick up errors like putting 'there' instead of 'their'. Proof-reading the work is very important.

It was a warm lovely day as Mina walked through her nice sweet smelling garden.

reading and enter them in a screen word bank using a program such as *Clicker* (Crick software) or *Inclusive Writer* (Inclusive Technology). Encourage your child to read the words and create his own sentences by clicking on the words in the correct order.

I have a pet Rabbit.

I	have	Dog Cat Fish
a	pet	

MAKING BOOKS FOR AGES 9–11

Often there is not enough time or computer access for children to produce longer pieces of writing at school. If your child is a keen storywriter he could develop a short chapter book over a period on the word processor at home. The book might be a continuation of a short story written at school or a sequel to a book he has read and enjoyed.

❑ Start by discussing the plot, the main characters, key events and how things are finally resolved.

❑ Teach your child how to justify the text, number the pages and centre titles.

Centre text

```
W Microsoft Word - Document1                               _ 6 X
File Edit View Insert Format Tools Table Window Help        _ 6 X
Normal    Times New Roman  14   B  I  U
```

Justify text

USING WORD BANKS

Support your child's reading by selecting some of the important words or phrases (e.g. names of characters, places, actions) from the book he is

For children who find reading and writing difficult, this type of program can help them put their ideas on paper and boost their confidence as writers. If they get tired of typing, they can dictate and you can type in the rest of the story. Children with learning disabilities can be helped to communicate using a word processor which includes a comprehensive range of symbols, such as *Writing with Symbols* (from Inclusive Technology).

LABELS AND LETTERS

These activities work for younger and older children. Help your child experiment with the word processor to make a label for his bedroom door.

How to do it

❑ Type in the words and highlight them.

❑ Select the Format **menu** from the top toolbar and click on *Font*.

❑ Choose the type of font you like, the size and colour.

❑ Experiment with borders, backgrounds and different type styles, e.g. outline or shadow.

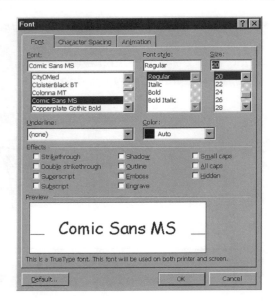

Most word processors have an address label facility. Get your child to print out name stickers for labelling her books, sports bag and other belongings, as follows:

- ❑ Click on *Tools*, then *Addresses* and *Labels*.
- ❑ Right click on the mouse to change the font for the label.
- ❑ Add decoration or a picture from the clip-art file.

Writing birthday thank you letters on the computer is a great way to show your child the power of word processing as a time saver! Together, make up a template letter so that you only need to change the name of the person you are addressing and the description of the present each time.

Dear **Will**
Thank you so much for the **puzzle** . I have had great fun playing with it.
Thanks for coming to my party.
Love from
Laura .

For young children, this takes the drudge out of writing thank you letters. However, it's important for older children to understand that word processing can make letters less personal. Part of learning about ICT is judging when there are better ways to do a task than using a computer.

A FAMILY NEWSPAPER (7 AND OLDER)

Make a Christmas or New Year surprise for friends and relatives. Children will enjoy using a word processing or **desktop publishing** program to create a newspaper featuring family events through the year. If you have a **scanner**, you can scan in photographs, drawings or cartoons. Otherwise you can contact a photo-processing company who will put an image of your photograph on CD for you, or you can use originals and make photocopies rather than printouts.

A SCHOOL – HOME TIMETABLE (7 AND OLDER)

Show your child how to use the table facility in the word processor. Together, make a timetable for the week, showing on which days he needs to take in the recorder, PE or swimming kit. Put in any after-school clubs or activities.

MONDAY	TUESDAY	WEDNESDAY	THURSDAY	FRIDAY
Recorder		PE	Swimming	
Reading book			Need packed lunch	Trip to Museum
	Chess club	Football club		

Typing tutor

Older children who are confident writers on paper can get frustrated trying to type with one or two fingers. Using typing tutor **software** can help and some types are specifically designed for children. However, do remember:

❑ If your child is reluctant to use the software, don't force him to do so.

❑ Only use it for short periods, about 15 minutes each time.

❑ This software helps to develop typing skills – not English or ICT.

EMAIL NET FRIENDS

Electronic mail (or **email**) is the **Internet's** same-day and (when it's working well) same-minute postal service. It is a great way to encourage children to write – they can send messages over the Internet to friends and relatives all over the world for the cost of a local phone call. Start by emailing friends you know well.

I've got mail! It must be from Lisa in California!

email hints

✧ Explain your family's email address to your child, or set one up especially for him.

User id	at	Domain name
toddfamily	@	example.co.uk

Pronounced: 'todd family at example dot co dot uk'

Save your phone costs

Compose your email off-line and connect to the Internet just to send the message. This will usually take less than a minute of phone time compared with many more minutes if you write your message when you are on-line.

You may know about a 'netiquette' that has built up amongst email users. Sending and getting email is like having an on-line conversation, except that you cannot see or hear one another. To add more meaning to the conversation, many people use 'smileys' in their emails. Here are a few examples which children will find fun to use.

Hold the book on its side to see the faces of these 'smileys':

:-)   Smiling

:- (Sad

;-)   Winking

:-S   Oops!

As well as smileys, and to save typing time, acronyms are often used as shorthand, e.g:

AAA (Any Advice Appreciated)

AVHBI (A Very Happy Bunny Indeed)

BTW (By The Way)

BBS (Be Back Soon)

TTFN (Ta Ta For Now)

Children can have fun making up their own.

Activities at home: Maths

Computers can give children the chance to work at a higher level in maths than they might normally do. This is because the software (e.g. a spreadsheet) does the tedious calculations, allowing more time for reasoning, i.e. working out what the results mean.

Some of the following activities show children how useful maths can be in everyday life, others that maths puzzles are fun to solve just for the sake of it!

SPREADSHEET ACTIVITIES

Spending plan (9-10)

Plan how to spend birthday money by using a **spreadsheet** to make calculations. Make a list of the items and how much they cost.

	A	B	C	D
1	Things to buy		Cost	
2				
3	Book		£ 4.99	
4	Felt pens		£ 2.50	
5	Lego		£ 7.99	
6				
7	Total		£ 15.48	
8				

How to do it

❑ Click on the first cell in the first column (cell A1) and type in the column label: 'Things to buy'.

❑ Type in any other labels, the items to buy and the prices in the other cells (as shown above).

❑ Fill cells in with different background colours to make the spreadsheet fun to look at.

❑ Get the spreadsheet to calculate the total, by clicking on the 'Total cost' cell

(cell C7 in the example) and then on the Σ symbol on the toolbar. The total cost will appear.

❑ If you are over budget, change some items and prices to bring the total within your budget.

Pocket money (10-11)

If you are confident in creating simple spreadsheets or are happy to learn from the on-line help, work with your child to set up a spreadsheet to keep track of her finances.

	A	B	C	D	E	F	G
1			03/01/00	10/01/00	17/01/00	24/01/00	31/01/00
2			Week 1	Week 2	Week 3	Week 4	Week 5
3	Income		£5.00	£1.50	£1.50	£1.50	£1.50
4	Earned		£0.50			£4.00	
5	Bt Fwd			£1.51	£3.01	-£3.48	£2.02
6	TOTAL		£5.50	£3.01	£4.51	£2.02	£3.52
7							
8	Spent :						
9	Books		£3.99				
10	Presents						
11	Clothes				£7.99		
12	Other						£0.99
13	TOTAL		£3.99	£0.00	£7.99	£0.00	£0.99
14	Balance		£1.51	£3.01	-£3.48	£2.02	£2.53
15							

In this example, the top rows record and total the money received and carried forward from the previous week. The lower rows record and add up the spending for that week, and subtract the total from the total income.

If your child is allowed to go into debt for something she especially wants, the spreadsheet would show a negative balance in red!

Encourage your child to use the spreadsheet for forward-planning. She can:

❑ Predict, then check how much money she will have built up in 6 months if she only spends 50p a week.

❑ Predict, then check how many weeks she would need to save all her pocket money to have enough to buy a new sweatshirt or a CD.

Doing this will help your child to understand real-life uses of the computer and to get used to spreadsheet skills.

Graph your growth (8-11)

Together, record your child's height on a spreadsheet like the one below. You could measure her height on her birthday, then every month or every three months. In this way, you can record, e.g. 8 years 3 months as 8.25 years, which makes it easier to graph. You can keep a record of any brother's and sister's heights too.

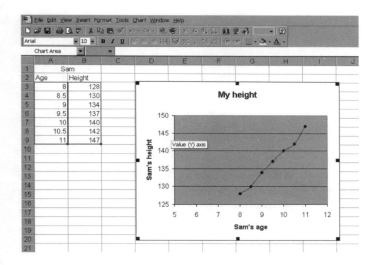

How to do it

❑ Highlight the age and height columns and display a graph. If you are using Excel, do this with the *Chartwizard* button.

❑ Select the scattergraph option with a line joining the points. Show your child how to label the chart axes and to give it a title.

❑ Experiment with changing the scale of the graph, so that it zooms in on the age-range you want to focus on.

ADVENTURE AND LOGIC GAMES

Good **adventure programs** are exciting and educational. They combine 3D photo-realistic graphics, sound and animation, and are best played together by parents and children who are six and older.

Most adventures share common elements such as a mission to find a person or to uncover a secret. As you explore your surroundings there are objects to note or collect, and puzzles to solve. This requires a logical approach to problem-solving and recording what you find. Encourage your child to keep a note of the paths you take and to draw careful maps of your route so that you can piece together the layout of the imaginary world you are exploring.

Don't expect your child to work on an adventure on her own. Good software of this kind is challenging and the educational value comes in comparing experiences with other adventurers.

Popular examples of this type of software includes *Zoombini Maths*, produced by Broderbund and suitable for 7-11 year-olds (KS2). It provides sequenced adventures with mathematical puzzles involving algebraic thinking and logical reasoning and is great for children to play with a friend. Another good game to play in pairs or groups is *Where in the World is Carmen Sandiego?* which combines logic and geography.

Of the hundreds of computer games available, *Myst* and its sequel *Riven* by Broderbund are very successful mystery adventures which are non-violent and suitable for families. The graphics and content are sophisticated and full of challenging puzzles. Children as young as 10 can enjoy the challenge and excitement of this type of adventure, but will need to work with parents or older siblings.

LOGO adventures

If your child enjoys the maths program LOGO, she could use it to write her own simple adventure game with help and ideas from the LOGO websites (see page 29).

SIMULATIONS

Simulation programs let children test out a model of a system such as plant growth, the water cycle or the development of a settlement. A popular type of simulation to use at home is one where you build and then run a town, e.g. *Simtown* (produced by Maxis).

With this type of program you and your child can work out the best strategy for keeping the town running smoothly, e.g. where to build roads, shops and schools, the effects of pollution and waste disposal, and the importance of work, education and leisure.

If you have a 10-11 year old who is interested in the history of the world, and you are looking for a stretching and challenging program, try the *Civilisation* family of strategy games (by Firaxis). These are adult games, so working on them would need to be a joint effort, otherwise your child may soon lose heart.

PRACTISING NUMERACY SKILLS

There are many maths practice programs available, but the quality varies. Some may appear bright and lively but in fact may become tedious and have questionable mathematical value. The following provide an enjoyable way to practice maths facts and skills:

Maths Workshop (by Broderbund) gives practice in the four rules (+ − x ÷) and fractions and also has activities to develop spatial skills (geometry). It is also worth looking at software produced by Doring Kindersley, Granada Learning and Edmark. You can often get a preview of software by looking at the company websites. Remember, you could ask your child's teacher or the school's ICT coordinator for recommendations of suitable software.

Checklist for numeracy software:

- ✧ Are the graphics interesting and of high quality?
- ✧ Are the graphics used to help explain the maths ideas? Are there different levels of difficulty?
- ✧ Can you move through the activities at a reasonable pace, or do you have to wait too long for the graphics or animation to catch up with you?
- ✧ Does the program monitor the mistakes made and give more practise at the same level?
- ✧ If the program tries to 'teach' methods of calculation, do these match the strategies taught in your child's school in the Numeracy curriculum?

It's a good idea to borrow software from a library or rent it from a multimedia centre, e.g. a video hire shop, to try before buying.

Activities at home: Designing

Designing on the computer builds up creative skills and style as well as being fun. You can choose from a range of software for designing printed material: word processors, painting programs, (e.g. *KidPix* by Broderbund), desktop publishers (e.g. Microsoft *Publisher*), and more specialist home publishing software (e.g. *PrintArtist* by Sierra, *Greetings Workshop* from Microsoft). Most of this software comes with a range of clip-art.

GREETINGS CARDS

Draw your own picture using a painting program and add a personal message. Print it out and stick it on the front of a folded piece of card. Alternatively, your software may print a cover and an inside message on an A4 sheet so that it can be folded in half and then in half again to make a card.

CALENDARS

Make a personal calendar for everyone in the family. Your child could create it from scratch using the table facility in the **word processor** and add **clip-art** and borders. Alternatively, many publishing programs have ready-made versions for you to customise.

❀ Mum's Calendar for June 2001 ❀						
Sun	Mon	Tue	Wed	Thur	Fri	Sat
					1	2
3	4	5	6	7	8	9
10	11	12	13	14	15	16
17	18	19	20	21	22	23
24	25	26	27	28	29	30

REPEAT PICTURES

Use a painting program such as KidPix

- ❑ Paint a self-portrait, using black outline and fill in the areas with bold colour.
- ❑ Save and print your first self-portrait.
- ❑ Now change the colours and print another version.
- ❑ Repeat this with different colour combinations until you have 4 versions of the same design.
- ❑ Mount these together on a large sheet of card.

MULTIMEDIA

The word multimedia describes screen pages that contain a mixture of words, pictures, sound and perhaps video clips or animation sequences.

Hot spots are set up in different areas of the screen page and when you click on them a sound clip could play or you might go to a new page.

'Happy Birthday' multimedia screen

Create a simple multimedia screen and wish someone in the family a happy birthday.

✧ **Use the sound recorder to record a birthday song or message.**

You will usually get to the sound recorder program by clicking through the following:

- ❏ *Start*
- ❏ *Programs*
- ❏ *Accessories*
- ❏ Either *Multimedia* or *Leisure*, or another similar folder
- ❏ *Sound Recorder*

(If you cannot find it, use the *Find* facility on the *Start* **menu.**)

Plug in the microphone and click on the red record button to start recording.

✧ **Type in a message in *Word Art*:**
- ❏ Click on the *Drawing* button on the Word toolbar.

❏ The Word Art window will open on screen, and you will be taken through the steps: choose a style of writing, then type in your message selecting the type and size of font.

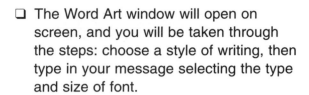

❏ Add a picture you've drawn in a graphics program or find a clip-art picture you like. Do this from the *Insert* menu by selecting *Picture* then *Clip-art* or *From File.*

❏ To insert your sound message click on the *Insert* menu then on *Object*, then *Select from File* and finally *Browse*. Find your recording from the file and insert it in your document.

❏ A sound file symbol

 **Click here**

will appear on screen. Double click on it to hear the sound.

Drawing button

❏ Click on the *Insert WordArt* icon on the drawing toolbar.

Insert WordArt button

AN 'ALL SINGING ALL DANCING' MULTIMEDIA PRESENTATION

If you have a package such as HyperStudio (distributed by TAG), you can work on a joint project with your child to create a simple multimedia presentation of a special occasion such as a birthday or holiday.

When you get family photos developed, ask the processors to put a copy on to CD-ROM for you.

Plan it on paper first.

❏ Start by creating one page with a small amount of text and a picture.

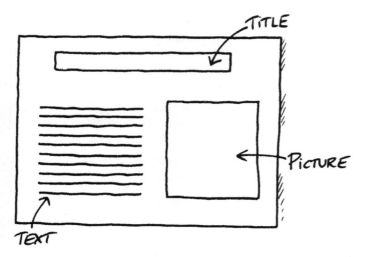

❏ Create a second page with a few lines of text, a picture, and sound that can be activated by clicking on a button.

❏ Pages can be linked by inserting a hot spot or button that is set to take the user to a different page. This can be visible or hidden behind a picture or text.

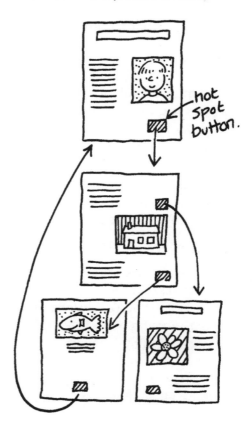

❏ It is important to plan on paper how the pages will link.

CREATE A WEBSITE

You can transfer a Hyperstudio presentation into a **website**, or create your own with a program such as *Hotdog Express* (by Sausage software) or *Site Central* (by Roger Wagner from TAG) which are easy enough for KS2 children to use.

Choose an **Internet Service Provider** (ISP) which allows you to publish a small website free. Most ISPs do so and will give you an address for your page(s), and on-line help on how to 'upload' your pages on to the web from your ISP.

For more information on the **Internet**, see page 27.

Activities at home: Research

Many parents are prompted to buy a computer 'to help with homework'. You can also help your child build up her general knowledge and her research skills by using the computer together to find information.

HOMEWORK

The software most useful for homework tasks are a **word processor**, reference **CD-ROMs** and the **Internet**. If your child has a piece of writing to do for homework, check that the purpose is not to practice handwriting before she uses the word processor! Keep the first draft as well as the final version – the teacher will find it useful to see the way your child has developed her work.

'Finding out' from CD-ROMs

A comprehensive CD-ROM encyclopaedia is an excellent investment. There are many titles available (e.g. Hutchinson's *Multimedia Encyclopaedia*, *Encarta* by Microsoft, *Europress Family Encyclopaedia* by Ransom). Be aware that they are updated yearly, so check when you buy whether a new edition is about to be launched. Some titles offer free on-line updates on world events, via the Internet.

You will need to help your child to find her way around the **software**, and to learn how to search an encyclopaedia for information. Encourage your child to identify the key words in the question she is asking.

To begin with, encourage her to make written notes on what she finds out. Some software includes a 'note taking' facility which older children could try.

Some CD-ROM encyclopaedias include a world atlas. As well as maps, many offer 'virtual flights' over the landscape to zoom in on for a close-up view.

Trace your family tree

Software such as *Family Tree Maker* (by Broderbund) gives you a structure to build your family tree and access to valuable census information. The Internet has a number of sites dedicated to genealogy and is a fascinating way to follow-up leads and trace long-lost relations.

Plan your holiday

Locate your holiday destination on a CD-ROM atlas and print out a map to help you plan your route. Look for more information on places of interest – beaches, theme parks, swimming pools, and so on – and put the information into a family 'holiday diary'. Look on the Internet for information, too.

PARENTS' INFORMATION NETWORK

The Parents' Information Network (www.pin-parents.com) was set up to provide information to parents on good use of computers. Their website contains advice on software and hardware, information about their publications and on-line software reviews and also offers help with homework.

ABOUT THE INTERNET

The Internet was started in the 1960s as an international network of computers that could communicate for military purposes. Since then the 'Net' has expanded to include thousands of different networks connecting millions of computers. Today, any computer can be linked to the Internet through an ordinary telephone line.

This is what you need to get connected:

- ❏ A computer and telephone line.
- ❏ A **modem** – usually the faster the better, but a modem speed of 56K should be adequate for ordinary home use.
- ❏ An Internet Service Provider (ISP). There are many free ISPs, e.g. FreeServe, UK Online, Virgin, Tesco, Waitrose. Although there is no subscription charge, beware that some of these ISPs charge for technical support.

This is what you need to surf the web:

- ❏ An Internet browser to search the World Wide Web. *Internet Explorer* and *Netscape Navigator* are the most popular and both are available free. Your ISP should provide you with a browser, but you may like to try alternatives. They are often offered free with computer magazines.

**Netscape Navigator
www.netscapeonline.co.uk**

Remember

Some damaging computer **viruses** can be picked up unknowingly by browsing the Internet and downloading information on to your home computer. Make sure you have virus checking software installed on your machine (e.g. *Dr Solomon's* or *Norton's Anti-Virus*).

TEACH YOUR CHILD THE BASICS OF WEB-BROWSING

Even if you are a confident user, remember that your child is not, so take things step-by-step.

- ❏ Connect to the Internet via your browser (e.g. double click on the *Internet Explorer* icon on your desktop).
- ❏ Choose a **search engine**, e.g. *Yahooligans* is specifically for children's sites.
- ❏ Type a key word or website address into the search engine's text box and click on search.
- ❏ If you are using key words, narrow down your search by:
  - ❏ Using capital letters at the beginning of proper names, e.g. London.
  - ❏ Putting quotation marks around complete phrases, e.g. 'medieval castles'.
  - ❏ Using more than one key word in order of importance. Type '+' in front of a word that must be included.

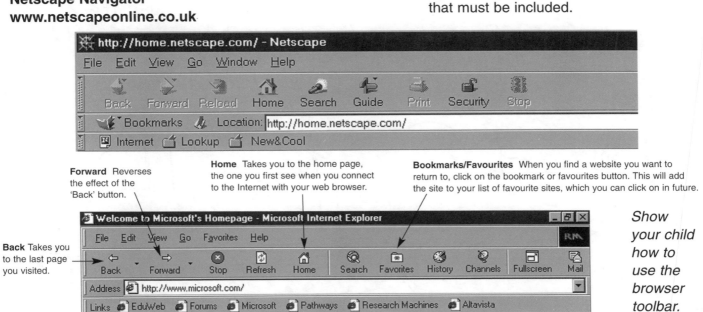

Forward Reverses the effect of the 'Back' button.

Home Takes you to the home page, the one you first see when you connect to the Internet with your web browser.

Bookmarks/Favourites When you find a website you want to return to, click on the bookmark or favourites button. This will add the site to your list of favourite sites, which you can click on in future.

Back Takes you to the last page you visited.

Show your child how to use the browser toolbar.

❏ Use the search engine's on-line help to try more complicated searches. If you do not find what you are looking for, try a different search engine.

Remember to **bookmark** sites you will want to find again.

❏ On the website contents page, show your child how to click on the areas indicated (i.e. where there is blue text, or the pointer changes to a hand icon) to take her on to more detailed pages.

Undesirable sites

Always be on hand when your child is using the Internet. You can install filter software (see page 29) to prevent accidentally reaching an undesirable site, but be aware that this is not absolutely foolproof.

SEARCH SUGGESTIONS

Information for homework and school projects:

EduWeb is an educational website (http:// www.eduweb.co.uk) which has links to a wide range of information on school projects.

The Parents Information Network (PIN) has a *Help with Homework* area on its website (http://www.pin-parents.com/learning/homhelp.htm) which provides links to sites, such as the *Mad Scientist Network* in which children can ask 'real' scientists their questions.

Many university websites have excellent web pages of information for children. Try the *Fibonacci Numbers* and the *Golden Section sites* (www.ee.surrey.ac.uk/Personal/RKnott/ Fibonaacci/fib.html).

On-line clubs

Mathematical Enrichment – NRICH (http:// www.nrich.amaths.org) is a maths site with games, puzzles and challenges, and the chance to make friends with other young maths enthusiasts.

Young Writers (http://kidpub.org/kidpub/). Your child can publish her story on the web and have fun reading other children's work.

On-line booksellers

Let your child choose books on-line and order them from Amazon (http://www.amazon.co.uk) Dillons (http://www.dillons.co.uk) or Waterstones (http://www.waterstones.co.uk).

Wow! This website is brilliant. I just typed in 'space exploration' and now I've reached Mars!

Useful resources

NB: All web addresses are up to date at the time of publication.

SOFTWARE & HARDWARE SUPPLIERS

Broderbund
www.broderbund.com
Distributed in UK by TAG, REM
Primary software including Living Books, Zoombinis

Crick Software
01604 671691
www.cricksoft.com
Clicker software

Dorling Kindersley Family Learning
www.dkonline.com
Home and education software

Eidos
www.eidosinteractive.com
Forestia software

Granada Learning
0161 827 2887
www.granada-learning.com
Primary curriculum software

Inclusive Technology
01457 819790
www.inclusive.co.uk
Primary and special needs software, e.g. Inclusive Writer, Writing with Symbols

Lingua Language Services
01484 689494
www.lingua-uk.com
Multilingual fonts for wordprocessing (Global Writer)

Logotron Educational software
01223 425558
www.logo.com
Primary curriculum software including a good version of LOGO, Superlogo

Maxis
020 7250 0215
www.simcity.com
Simulation software, e.g. Simtown

Mindscape
www.mindscape.com
Software for children and adults, e.g. Mavis Beacon Teaches Typing

Research Machines
01235 826000
www.rm.com
Primary curriculum software, hardware, e.g. small (infant) mouse, graphics tablet

Rickitt Educational Media
01458 254700
www.r-e-m.co.uk
Primary curriculum software retailer, offering a comprehensive listing of titles in their 'Educational Software Yearbook'

Sierra
www.sierra-online.co.uk

TAG (distributor)
0800 591262
www.tagdev.co.uk
Primary curriculum software

Topologika
01326 377771
www.topolgka.demon.co.uk
Primary literacy and numeracy software

USEFUL SOFTWARE

Keyboard skills
Type to Learn (7-adult) Sunburst, TAG
Mavis Beacon Teaches Typing (8-adult) Mindscape

Publishing software
Print Artist Plus Sierra
KidPix Studio Broderbund

Website safeguards (downloaded free):
Net Nanny www.netnanny.co.uk
Cyber Patrol www.cyberpatrol.com
Surf Watch www.surfwatch.com
Netpilot www.equinet.com

INFORMATION FOR PARENTS

Parents Information Network
0870 60 40 231
www.pin-parents.com

Primary education websites

British Education Communications Agency
www.becta.org.uk
Literacy, Numeracy and other curriculum schemes
www.standards.dfee.gov.uk
National Grid for Learning www.ngfl.uk
Ofsted www.ofsted.gov.uk
Qualifications and Curriculum Agency
open.gov.uk/qca
RM education content service www.eduweb.co.uk

CD-ROMS

Here is a small selection of good educational
CD-ROMS. More titles are published each year.

Reference

Children's Encyclopaedia (7-11) Dorling Kindersley
Encarta World Atlas (all ages) Microsoft
Eyewitness World Atlas (12+) Dorling Kindersley
My First Dictionary (3-7) Dorling Kindersley

English

I Love Spelling (7-11) Dorling Kindersley
*Living Books: The Tortoise and the Hare, Just Grandma
and Me, Darby the Dragon* (5-10) Broderbund
Mad about English 1 and *2* (7-11) Dorling Kindersley
(spelling and wordbuilding practice)
Sherlock (5-11)Topologika

Maths/Numeracy

Carmen Sandiego – Maths Detective (7+) Broderbund
I Love Maths (7-11) Dorling Kindersley
Maths Explorer (7-11) Granada Learning
Maths Workshop (5-11) Broderbund
Megamaths (5-11) Logotron
SuperLogo (7+) Logotron
Zoombini Maths/Logical Journey of the Zoombinis (7-11)
Broderbund

Science

Forestia (7-11) Eidos (nature adventure)
Magic School Bus: Dinosaurs (5-10) Microsoft
My Amazing Human Body (5-10)
My First Amazing Science Explorer (5-9) Dorling Kindersley
Science Explorer 1 & 2 (7+) Granada Learning
The Ultimate Human Body (10+) Dorling Kindersley
The Way things Work (7+) Dorling Kindersley

History

Castle Explorer (7-11) Dorling Kindersley
Eyewitness History of the World (7+) Dorling Kindersley
My First Amazing History Explorer (5-9) Dorling Kindersley

Geography

Encarta 2000 World Atlas (all ages) Microsoft
Interactive Atlas of Great Britain (7-adult) Ordnance Survey
My First Amazing British Isles Explorer (5-9) Dorling
Kindersley
Where in the World is Carmen Sandiego? (7+) Broderbund

INTERNET SITES

Children's websites

BBC www.bbc.co.uk

Blue Peter www.bbc.co.uk/bluepeter/

Encyclopaedia Britannica Internet Guide www.eblast.com

How Stuff Works www.howstuffworks.com/

KidsZone freezone.com/

Knowledge Adventure http://www.adventure.com/
(mainly US sites)

LEGO www.LEGO.com/

Nrich Maths challenges www.nrich.amaths.org

The Disney site www.disney.com

The Natural History Museum www.nhm.ac.uk/

Young writers http://kidpub.org/kidpub/

Welcome to the Planets http://pds.jpl.nasa.gov/planets/

Other sites

British museums – plans, summary of contents
http://www.mda.org.uk/vlmp

Logo-type software (to download) www.lcsi.ca and
www.microworlds.com

National Geographic www.nationalgeographic.com

On-line encyclopaedia www.encyclopaedia.com

Shakespeare www.shakespeare.org.uk

The British Library http://portico.bl.uk

'The Earth and Moon Viewer'
www.fourmilab.ch/earthview/vplanet.html

Times Educational Supplement – Educational website
www.learnfree.co.uk

Weather information
www.bbc.co.uk/weather/index.shtml

USEFUL BOOKS

Buying a computer and printer (Parents Information
Network)

Computers Unlimited (super.activ series) by
Lisa Hughes (Hodder Children's Books, 1998)

The Internet (super.activ series) by
Lisa Hughes (Hodder Children's Books, 1998)

Your Own Website (super.activ series) by
Bill Thompson (Hodder Children's Books, 1999)

Definitive Guide to the Internet by Paul Bartlett (1999)

101 things to do with your computer (Usborne, 1998)

101 things to do on the Internet (Usborne, 1998)

Educational Software Handbook
(Parents Information Network)

Glossary

Adventure program Program in which the user explores a fantasy environment to solve a puzzle or mystery.

Apple Macintosh Make of computer that uses a different system to a PC.

Art program Program for drawing and painting.

Bookmarks (or **Favourites**) Links which go directly to your favourite websites.

Bytes Units of computer memory: 1 MB (megabyte) = 1 million bytes; 1 GB (gigabyte) = 1000 MB.

CD-ROM Software on a disk which can contain text, sound, pictures and video.

Clip-art Ready-to-use images available on CD-ROM, the Internet or installed on a computer.

Computer program (or **software**) Set of instructions which makes the computer work.

Configure Adjust a computer feature (e.g. the mouse speed).

Database Data organised into records that can be easily searched.

Desktop publisher Program for laying out text and pictures, e.g. to make a newsheet.

Download Transfer a document from the Internet to your own computer.

Email Messages sent from computer to computer via the Internet.

File Text document or picture held on the hard disk.

Floor robot Battery-operated dome- or box-shaped robot with a keypad for keying in instructions.

Floppy disk Disk used to hold software and documents.

Folder Area on the hard disk set up to organise a collection of files.

Graphing program Program which displays typed data in different formats, e.g. bar chart, line graph.

Hard disk The storage disk inside the computer which holds permanent file copies.

Hardware The physical parts of a computer system, e.g. keyboard, monitor, printer.

Internet A worldwide computer network.

ISP (**Internet Service Provider**) Company which provides a link to the Internet.

LOGO Simple programming language for children.

Memory Computer storage area which runs the software. The bigger the memory, the more the computer can do.

Menu List of choices in a program often shown in a menu bar at the top of the screen.

MODEM Device which converts computer data into signals that can be sent down a telephone line to send email or connect to the Internet.

Multimedia program Program which can run on a multimedia computer and includes, text, sound, pictures and video.

National Grid for Learning Interconnecting computer networks which support teaching, learning, training and administration in schools, colleges, universities, libraries, the workplace and homes.

Network Several computers linked together that can share equipment, e.g. a printer, and transfer documents between them.

PC (personal computer) Most commonly used computer type, with an IBM-compatible system.

Processor speed The speed at which a computer works, measured in megahertz.

Programming Creating a set of instructions to make a computer complete a task.

Save Make a permanent copy of a file on the computer's hard disk.

Scanner Equipment which copies a picture or printed document into the computer.

Search engine Program which searches a huge database of websites.

Simulation program Educational program which models a process, e.g. the water cycle, and shows the result of changes to the process.

Software A computer program.

Software bundle Collection of computer programs.

Spreadsheet Program for calculating data.

Virus Hidden program which can corrupt a computer.

Web browser Program for reading web pages.

Web page Document published on the World Wide Web.

Website Collection of linked web pages.

Word processor A writing program.

World Wide Web (**WWW**) Collection of websites and the movement between them on the Internet.

Index

Activities

ISBN 0 340 77820 2

10 9 8 7 6 5 4 3 2 1

Text copyright © 2000 Sharon Harrison

Illustrations copyright © 2000 Sascha Lipscomb

The right of Sharon Harrison and Sascha Lipscomb to be identified as the author and illustrator of this work has been asserted by them in accordance with the Copyright, Design and Patents Act 1988.

Published by Hodder Children's Books, a division of Hodder Headline, 338 Euston Road, London NW1 3BH

Printed and bound in Great Britain.

A CIP record is registered by and held at the British Library.